A Black Girl with the Blues

By Sarah Porter-Liddell

The contents of this work, including, but not limited to, the accuracy of events, people, and places depicted; opinions expressed; permission to use previously published materials included; and any advice given or actions advocated are solely the responsibility of the author, who assumes all liability for said work and indemnifies the publisher against any claims stemming from publication of the work.

All Rights Reserved
Copyright © 2023 by Sarah Porter-Liddell

No part of this book may be reproduced or transmitted, downloaded, distributed, reverse engineered, or stored in or introduced into any information storage and retrieval system, in any form or by any means, including photocopying and recording, whether electronic or mechanical, now known or hereinafter invented without permission in writing from the publisher.

Dorrance Publishing Co
585 Alpha Drive
Pittsburgh, PA 15238
Visit our website at *www.dorrancebookstore.com*

ISBN: 979-8-8868-3061-3
eISBN: 979-8-8868-3925-8

Note to my readers:

This work isn't pretty. I went through the worst, and longest, depression of my life (thus far); it lasted nearly seven months. This is how I survived. This is what I had to say.

Trigger warnings: suicide, depression, body dysmorphia, anxiety

Death is inevitable
and somehow, all the things that feel large, overwhelming, and painful—seem small.
We spend most of our lives worrying about things that we won't remember. We don't even live our lives. And then we die. Not remembering a single thing that worried us, but remembering all the things we wish we had done. We've got to collect our flowers now.

Cattle

I imagine cattle know they're going to die
before they feel the barrel of a cold stunner
pressed against their foreheads. The anxiety
of the other cows overwhelms them all
when they're forced into a single-file line
and marched into isolation.
Huddled closely together, their bodies shiver,
tears run along the lids of their eyes; their cries unheard.

A single cow,
shoved forward assumes a sense of pride and humility,
before an iron gate closes behind him; the others
watch in silence—relieved
they haven't yet been chosen. Standing alone,
the cow looks straight ahead,
metal pressed into his forehead; he doesn't blink.
Blood runs down his face,
pieces of him splatter on a wooden board behind him,
his body falls heavily to the ground.

I asked a black man,
lying restlessly next to me,
about love—about
the love he has for me,
the love for anything.
He doesn't blink.
He looks aimlessly into the sky,
he avoids me;

avoids my question and chuckles. Confused,
I move closer, lying my head on his chest.
"Tell me," I whisper delicately near his ear.
His chest heaves in and out, quickly; he's anxious.
I feel uneasy begging for attention.

He gets out of bed.
Light from my bedroom window darkens the lines on his face;
he is beautiful and melancholy.
I watch him walk slowly to the bathroom,
run water across his face, and avoid
looking in the mirror too long. He dresses
without acknowledging me; exits without goodbye.

When he leaves, cold wind hits him, a grimace,
permanently frozen to his face.
No obvious danger present, he walks—head down,
hood up, hands in his pockets.
Cars hunk loudly, voices high within the noise;
he feels uneasy.
He's pushed forward by a crowd of men behind him,
he is isolated along the wall. The wail
of a loud siren freezing him.
He doesn't blink.
Hands against the wall.
"I didn't do nothin'."

The last time I cried,
I asked myself why I was crying.
I've given myself this expectation—strength is not a luxury, but a necessity.
I've lost my ability to feel—when I need to feel, for me.
I've convinced myself I need to earn my tears.
My pains aren't actually pain.
And at some point, I need to have all of my shit together—and having your shit together means that you don't require support.
That's toxic strength.

The world has convinced me that my value is related to my ability to achieve, to perform, to solve problems.
And as a black woman,
my womanhood is not defined by having children, or a successful career, education, or even a family—but the value of my work ethic. How much I can handle?
How much can I handle?
I'm valued by how much I can handle without breaking, without crying,
without showing weakness.

A Black Girl with the Blues

I'm still conditioned to stand on a wooden block, in front of crowd, and be examined for my strength. Everyone's expectations.
And without anyone ever opening their mouth I've learned that my place is earned by what I can contribute, without asking for anyone to give anything back.

I stopped crying.

Am I supposed to be unhappy?
I don't ask for anything, so I get nothing.
Closed mouths don't get fed...but, when do we anticipate the needs of our loved ones? Do we ever get to a place where our mouths never have to open and we still get fed?
Am I unworthy or unattractive?
I can't keep feeling like this.
I'm tired of crying.
Feeling alone. Worrying
about everything. I'm
tired.

A Black Girl with the Blues

When people ask
"*How are you?*" Many of them don't wait to hear your response
before they fix their mouths to say, "*That's great to hear.*"
They just know you'll say you're "okay."

How would it feel?
To genuinely be asked "How are you?" and to watch the person wait,
in actual anticipation of an answer.
To witness them caring about your response and wanting to know with certainty that your "I'm okay" is not just an "okay" for "okay sakes." But your "okay" is an "okay" not a "great" but an "okay" and that means that they can be okay with your answer.

Our days move quickly. We get consumed by ourselves, the people we love, the people we love and care for, the people we only care for,
and then with the everyday—everyday.
Do we stop to see if we're okay?

Do we just say we're okay? Are you okay—today?
Any day?

Feeling down tonight

Turning thirty and just can't even think of a future.
I can't afford a home.
Someone said I was supposed to own a home by now.

I'm too intimidating to date.
So, I'm not meeting anyone.
Someone said I was supposed to married by now.

I'm struggling,
with motivation for this dissertation.
Someone said I was supposed to be a doctor by now.

And I'm too fat.
Someone said I don't have kids, I should be smaller now.

All I feel like I do is complain to myself.
I lose weight, I gain it back.
I save. I spend it.
I date.
I lose interest.

I just want to experience things.
A romance. Some traveling.
I just don't want to worry anymore.

Cheryl Lynn
Encore.
On repeat. I'm so lonely tonight—
first weekend in over a month,
I'll be spending alone.
Someone I've grown to love, is not even fighting
to keep me.
Reminded of how easily it truly is, not to need me.
Not to miss me.
I don't know…

I changed the home screen on my phone;
it used to be a picture of Duke and Fitz. That was hard. But I did it. Doesn't change how my heart feels. Doesn't change the void I feel. Doesn't change the loneliness I feel. Doesn't change that I know people don't care. They don't think losing a pet is difficult.
It's okay, though.
The PCOS has taken time off my miserable life. And with my luck? I'll get tired of taking the medicine and just die. I realize I'm too scared to commit suicide. I want to die though, at least I think I do.
Will I ever not feel this way?
Will it be too late if I ever finally do?

Epiphany
All I've ever known is my own effort. As I think on my childhood, I now realize—my feelings never mattered. As an adult, my experience doesn't matter. I literally... don't matter. Unless. I'm doing something for someone else. I can't live like this anymore

Every weekend,
I try to make some time for you, and things seem fine.
And then, every week, I go Monday to Thursday without hearing from you. Things would be so much easier for me if I was interested in someone else. And I know you don't care for me the way I care for you.
I'm stupid for even dealing with any of this. But this loneliness I feel
is like a void. And the only time I feel okay
is when I'm around you.
But. You just get to do your own thing.
Talk to whoever, sleep with whoever, and pretend like this will be more than it is. And I just can't keep doing that.
If there was a way to get you out of my system quickly, I would have done it.
But week after week I feel myself always giving in,
the moment you text me.
I've got to stop doing that.
I'm not benefiting from this situation, and at this point, neither are you.
So, what's the point?

Do I even exist?
I keep asking myself this question,
because I feel invisible...
I mean, unless I'm having sex.
I don't feel seen. Valued. Or heard.
And I guess, I'm just wondering, if I have any value left—
that creates an existential dread. I don't feel like it matters
if I'm alive, because all I do is give—even when no one
thinks I am. I'm only living because I'm scared to die.
I'm only scared to die because I'm scared of Hell. I'm only
scared of Hell because it's eternal. I'm subconsciously
unable to commit to anything,
because I hope I'm going to die.

Everything makes me sad
I can't make this up. How I look. My finances. Where I live. Being a nobody. My body. My hair. My skin. Just Everything. I feel more inclined to die every day. And without Duke here, getting Regina healthy is the only thing keeping me here. Pathetic. I'm aware.

Everyday,
I'm literally fighting for my life. Most days, I want to die.
Even when I'm having a "good day,"
I want to die. I just get scared.
I don't want to go to Hell.
But if there was any certainty that I wouldn't go to Hell,
I'd like to die now. Peacefully.
After I finally stop crying and fall asleep,
 I'd like to never wake back up.
But my soul would travel to heaven. And if God will allow,
I'd watch and continue to pray for my family, from above.
I'm tired.

FB posts
I keep making posts so people will think I'm okay. I'm…ok.

> Some of us have gotten so used to hurting, we're afraid to heal. Forgive yourself for not loving yourself, and then you'll forgive others for not loving you properly. Give yourself the same grace you extend to others. You can't keep pouring into other people's cups and not filling yours back up. Learn to identify your own demons. Everyone is not your enemy. If you don't want me to overthink, you need to give me the details.
>
> Stop telling all your business to everybody; some people aren't listening to help; sometimes they're looking for you to fail. It's okay to love again. Don't forget that.
>
> Stop telling me I'm sensitive because I expect you to respect how I feel.
>
> If I have to ask you where I fit in your life, you're not making room. I'm not begging for anyone's attention anymore. If you're not making time for me, you're showing me how you feel about me.

If you matter to yourself, don't let anyone else make you feel like you don't.

People can make you feel like you're going crazy because you're evolving. Don't let people hold you back because they aren't meant to be where you're headed.

If you want to change it,
change it.
This is a universal motto that people tell you in a time of despair.
People think if you're complaining about it—fix it.
It's that simple. Get up, find the energy you need to fix the thing that is causing you grief. "Eat the frog," they say.
Do the hardest thing of the day—everything else will seem easy in comparison.
What if,
I'm the hard thing of the day? What if,
my existence—simply my being alive,
or taking up space, or drawing breath,
is the most difficult thing I need to do for the day?

Is it an accomplishment that I opened my eyes?

I was called impressive.
That made me blush.
Now, I just want to disappear.

I've been writing,
as long as I can...remember,
and I've never been that "good."
As a teenager, I wrote poetry.
I even took on performance poetry by joining an after-school club. The teachers and coaches were amazed by my work, but I felt lackluster in comparison to my friends. No one was going out of their way to make sure I felt supported, or asking me where I was hoping my writing would take me.

It wasn't until Georgia Me, a famous performance poet from Atlanta, was a special guest in our after-school class, that I learned people wanted to hear from me. Georgia encouraged me to perform in our school's open mic. At her request, I did. I stood—for the very first time—fifteen years old, in front of an entire gym of judgmental kids—and read my poem. The clapping, and yelling when I finished, was overwhelming. I'd never felt more confident.

Georgia was standing behind the stage when I finished performing. She told me, "You're amazing, but you need to get off that paper." She was referring to the printed copy of the poem I was reading on stage. I realized then, I had to memorize my work to be taken seriously.

I want to be taken seriously.

A Black Girl with the Blues

I've got to change,
My life.

I've never had actual support;
just people who watch me from a distance, and tell me they're proud when I accomplishsomething new.

But, I don't feel accomplished.
I feel like I'm sinking, and there is some plan I'm missing out on because I'm trying to make it day by day.

Tomorrow, I'm going to try something new.
I'm going to bet on me.
I did it before, and for my current position—this time, I'm shooting beyond my career.

These next few years are for me.

I'm counting my wins.
I've spent too much time counting my losses crying and watching others move on—move up, move out, and be renewed with energy I thought I'd never have.

I stopped doing that.

Today, I made a student who felt the world was crushing them smile and agree to create a haunted house. They thought they would never be able to be involved on campus, and now they can't wait to get started. That's a win.

Colleagues told me "thank you." They're so happy that difficult conversations are followed by action plans and have never felt more liberated in their ability to speak up. That's a win.

I advocated for myself.
Call that a win.

A Black Girl with the Blues

My dog smiled because she felt the warm sun on her thick coat for the first time in months. And I mean warm—seventy-three degrees.
She decided to lie on the porch and watch a flock of birds, smiling.
What a win?

It's taken me years to understand that wins matter as much as our losses. And if we don't celebrate them, if we don't acknowledge them, if we can't see them—we will always feel small, invisible, and alone.

I won today.

Sarah Porter-Liddell

I've got this existential dread,
around growing old.
I turned thirty in January of 2022,
and the world won't let me forget.
Older women are calling me old.
Younger women are calling me older,
and men are making me feel like I've done something wrong
by not already having children.

The gray hair has been there
since I was a child.
My first batch appeared at five years old.
I didn't really have the opportunity to be excited about
the gray hair meaning wisdom
—unless wisdom isn't defined by age—which was the
only thing making growing older exciting.

I don't drink coffee, juice,
or milk.
And don't eat much pork. I love sugar.
Cold weather. Sexy outfits. Sex.
Yes, I still get horny.
My body sometimes aches when I wake, but when I look
in the mirror, I never see the same woman.

A Black Girl with the Blues

Not because I've gotten older, but because I love myself differently. I've survived— differently.
Depression. I survived that.
Suicidal attempts. I've survived that.
Body dysmorphia and the war against fat people—
I'm surviving that.

I can't look in the mirror and not be proud of how my age defines my resilience. Something about knowing that my close encounters with death, and cheating death, feels rewarding, and I dare to say that there will be a time when I look at myself and find myself remarkable.

So, call me old.
Fill me with dread,
because I no longer understand the language of the youth.
Project your anguish with menopause and its hormonal changes at my thirty-year-old body, inexperienced to these things, because it is now all you can think about.
This is all okay.

Because one thing I've learned,
more than anything else—as cliché as it be—I keep surviving because
I want to see me.

We saved our friendship,
with an argument.
Today, I was so ready to dismiss this man—even though we had true chemistry, because my pride was hurt.

He hurt my feelings, without realizing he had, and for two hours straight we debated back and forth about being friends.

He texted me after I told him to take care, and called me out on not even giving a friendship a chance.
I guess I'm always worried about being worthy.

When will I get to a place where my emotions aren't the reason I feel vulnerable?

Hey, black girl
I see you. Feeling ignored.
Being told to be quiet. Being told only men lead.
Being told no one wants to marry you. Being asked not to make too much money. Being told to be okay making sacrifices.
Always making sacrifices.
Being measured by your strength. Being neglected.
Worrying about your skin getting too dark from the summer sun.
Worrying about your curl pattern being too tight.
Trying to avoid all the carbs, but wanting some baked mac and cheese, candied yams, and dressing to feed your soul.
Hiding in your pain.
Trying to hide accomplishments. Minimizing yourself so you don't seem too big in a room where you're clearly the brightest.

But black girls, I see you.
Dancing when you want to be crying. Solving world problems for people who have tried and failed.
Choosing love when it doesn't always choose you.
Making beautiful families. Choosing healing over anger.
Making healthy food choices when you want something else.

Sarah Porter-Liddell

Working out and finding peace. Seeking support.
Cutting your hair and redefining yourself.
Coloring your locs.
Living. Breathing. Smiling.
Working. Healing. Laughing.
Being you. Black Women. I see you.

I survived this thing,
a thing that felt inevitable,
held me captive on my living room couch.
Crying into a pillow I hadn't washed.
Lying on a blanket I wouldn't clean.
Petting a dog I was trying to connect with.
Smiling in my coworkers faces, every day.
Posting online so that people would know I was alive,
and lying about how I was feeling.

I survived this thing that made me hate myself,
beg for death. I prayed for death.
I'm glad God was listening with different ears.

I survived this thing
that told me I wasn't worthy,
had me crying about things I thought I'd healed from,
trying to define healing like it was something you just complete,
like healing isn't something you have to keep working on.
You have to keep working on that.

I survived this thing
and I'm still trying to define what "surviving really means.

Sarah Porter-Liddell

Maybe,
I need to stop that. I need to stop, defining things,
and accept them for what they are,
embrace how they make me feel, and keep
surviving.

You can.
you will,
survive this thing.